"A lovely book! Clear, gentle, and practical — just like the experience of meditation itself."

— Tobin Blake, author of *The Power of Stillness*

"Diana Lang's gift is her simplicity. She has the courage to demystify meditation and make it easily accessible, and she infuses her book with warmth, clarity, and gentleness. This is a fine and open-minded introduction to meditation that should suit many people of different persuasions."

— Andrew Weiss, author of *Beginning Mindfulness*

"Diana Lang understands the fears that block most people from meditating effectively. Her instructions on how to remove them are so simple and delightful that it almost seems unfair that we get results so quickly. Isn't meditation supposed to be daunting? But the benefits don't stop there. Lang also understands and gently leads us to the ultimate benefit — the experience of the loving Reality that already embraces us all."

— Gayle and Hugh Prather, authors of *Shining Through*

OPENING to MEDITATION

A Gentle, Guided Approach

dear dear Kat
my friend, my hero
I love you so much!
always & always
Diana Lang

A Book and CD Set

DIANA LANG

NEW WORLD LIBRARY
NOVATO, CALIFORNIA

New World Library
14 Pamaron Way
Novato, California 94949

Copyright © 2004 by Diana Lang

Edited by Marc Allen
Front cover design, text design, and typography by Mary Ann Casler
Author photo by J. Daniel Chapman
CD produced by Angela Hite
CD engineered and mastered by Jimmy Hite
Music by Martin Lund

Library of Congress Cataloging-in-Publication Data

Lang, Diana, 1957–
Opening to meditation : a gentle, guided approach / Diana Lang.— 1st ed.
          p.   cm.
"A book and CD set".
ISBN 1-57731-454-9 (pbk. : alk. paper)
1. Meditation. I. Title.
BF637.M4L36 2004
158.1´2—DC22

First printing, November 2004
ISBN 1-57731-454-9
Printed in China
Distributed to the trade by Publishers Group West

10 9 8 7 6 5 4 3 2 1

for june

breathe.

CONTENTS

PART I: the art of meditation

PART II: the practice of meditation

the art of meditation

P
A
R
T

O
N
E

CHAPTER 1

MEDITATION IS EASY

Meditation is easy. You can do it right now, right where you are. It is not mysterious or esoteric. It is your natural birthright as a human being.

Meditation is an age-old practice that quiets the mind and allows our inner spirit to shine through our life more and more. The effects of meditation unfold over time. It is a practice of awareness that increases our focus, our consciousness, and our soul-knowing.

Meditation creates a foundation that lets you know yourself deeply — your *true* self — the part of you that is eternal. It allows for the full potential of your soul to be expressed in your daily life.

Meditation helps you to become self-realized — to realize who you really are in your deepest essence. In meditation, you arrive at a state of awareness where you consciously recognize the link between your personality and your soul. Meditation aligns these two seemingly separate parts so they are known to be one and act as one. This is called *congruency* — a conscious bridge between the self and the soul.

The path to self-realization is a choice. It is the ongoing decision to live your life as truthfully and lovingly as possible. Every time you sit to meditate you are choosing to live an awakened life.

Meditation reveals a beauty beyond words. By turning within, we discover a world of knowledge, the bounty of our rich inner knowing. We discover that we are more than what we seem; we are better — far greater — than what we have believed about ourselves.

At our core, we discover we are simply and absolutely the radiance of pure love. Allowing this love to shine more brightly through our life is an inevitable and direct consequence of our meditation practice. We are the directors of our growth; it is always our choice to what degree we want to be receptive to our inner knowing. This inner knowing is always available to us. It does not waver or vary. The flow of our soul is constant. All we have to do is open to it.

CHAPTER 2

YOU ALREADY HAVE EVERYTHING YOU NEED

One of the purposes of this book is to show you that you need nothing outside yourself to take your next spiritual step. You already have everything you need.

Your next step is the one that's right in front of you, the one you can take right now. If you let your inner knowing guide you, you can't go wrong. Your next step almost always feels simple, natural, even ordinary. We sometimes expect great changes to happen in our lives instantly, in some dramatic fashion, with a bang, but that rarely happens. More often it is simply putting one foot in front of the other until inevitably some momentous event occurs; it looks like a miracle from the outside, but your personal experience of it most likely feels quite normal and natural. We're always looking for some breathtaking, heart-stopping spiritual event to know we've arrived, when in fact it is most often as ordinary as exhaling.

All it takes is an understanding of a few basic truths: we are far greater beings than we think we are. We have a vast and eternal spirit as well as these physical bodies. Where we are at this moment, how we are, who we are, is perfect as it is. There is no secret recipe; there is no magic formula. It is all as it should be, a perfect and gentle unfolding of your soul. If it feels difficult, it is only because you are out of touch with your true self; you are out of the flow.

When we're out of flow, we're out of sync with our soul. This creates a feeling of separation that in the moment feels real and true. When we feel separate, we are suffering from the painful illusion that we are unworthy in some way. This is a fallacy, perpetuated by our smaller self, or by what is often called the ego. It can throw us off course and confuse our sense of direction.

Meditation is a direct route to inner harmony, balance, and peace. There are many methods that can take you where you want to go, but meditation is by far the quickest and most precise. Its effects are cumulative and lasting. You can stop meditating for years and pick up right where you left off.

When this life is over, you won't take your possessions, your degrees, or your deeds with you, but you will take the consciousness you have built up from your meditation practice. Through your meditation, your consciousness changes and evolves. You become aware of who you really are. The consciousness you build in this lifetime is your ever-increasing legacy.

This consciousness is who you are.

CHAPTER 3

YOU ARE GOOD

Through the process of meditation you discover your true goodness. It may take a while, and you may have to wade through doubts and fears at first, but at some moment you'll discover — there at the core of you, perfectly in place — your authentic, worthy, beautiful self.

Anything that says otherwise is the ego's doubt, and if there's a devil, this is it. It causes us to confuse ourselves and forget who we really are. When we doubt, we empower fear. Doubt is at the heart of any fear-based decision — the decision to not trust, the decision to not be open, the decision to not love. Doubt is the stuff of our insecurity. It is at the core of any act that is less than our best.

Meditation helps you sift through all of this doubt and fear and feel your way home to your true self, to the knowing that you are naturally and inherently *good*. There are no exceptions. You are not the one exception.

What if you knew that?

What if it weren't even a question?

What if it were a given in your life?

Feel how much this would change how you express yourself in the world.

You are good — not in the sense of being righteous, of being superior to someone else, but in the deeper sense of it all, you are truly, heartfully good.

This is the truth. You are good beyond your wildest imagination. You are good in a way that is immeasurable. You are as worthy as your greatest hero or anyone that you have ever thought of as admirable, inspired, or blessed.

You are that.

Meditation is a journey that unifies the mind and the heart. Meditation uncovers the layers of belief, limitation, and doubt to quietly reveal the pure and simple heart that is always there.

I like to do things in the most direct way I can, as the crow flies, fast and true. Meditation is the most direct route home I know. It is a process, a discipline, an art, and a practice that will teach you to trust yourself, to come home within yourself, to know who you are, to be who you are, authentic and free and unlimited. Meditation will give you nothing new, but it will give you yourself.

CHAPTER 4

RIGHT WHERE
YOU ARE

The answers you are looking for can be found right where you are. Your point of power is in this present moment. It is so simple, yet it is true. All you need to do is know where you are in this moment to gain your orientation and sureness of footing. If you don't know where you actually are, all the good or even profound direction in the world could lead you far from your intended destination. If you don't know where you're standing, your aim will be far from the mark.

Meditation helps you know where you are in time and

space. It grounds you in the world so that you can move forward with fluidity and grace. Like a big red arrow on a map at the mall, it lets you know that YOU ARE HERE. When you understand where you actually are, the universe opens up with a thousand choices, each one unique and perfect in its own right, making it easy to know what your next step is.

All you have to do is open your heart to the light and energy that flows through us in every moment. That flow is always present; it is constant and perfect, always available to you. Imagine a stream of pure love outpouring from the universe straight into you. Imagine that same pure love flowing and dancing around and through every single thing on this planet and beyond this planet — every rock, every blade of grass, every deer in the forest, every star in the sky. Everything is connected to this flow.

And you are too.

The only reason we don't feel it is because we think that somehow we are separate from it. But we *are* it, and it is us. Feel it right now, in this very moment — let yourself open to the flow of love that is coursing through every single thing on this planet, through every single atom of every single one of us.

Meditation gives us an experience of this, so we feel it and know it deeply, beyond words. Meditation opens your mind and heart.

The opening of your heart is the most precious gift you can give the world. It affects everyone, and in this way meditation is also service, supporting the whole of humanity and all of life. As you become more aware, more conscious, you blaze the trail for the rest of us to follow, and our paths become much easier because of the steps you have taken. Know this, in your unfolding, in your deepening: that your inner journey creates an easier way for all of us.

By meditating we are opening into love. We enter a place that is sacred. By knowing where we are, we create an opening, a window to expanded consciousness. In that opening, we can feel and merge with the creative force of the universe. This cosmic creativity is simply love. We may call it God, or nature, or luck, or spirit, or universal energy, or a higher power, or something else. Whatever you call it, it is still love. Pure love. Love that intends; love that makes; love that builds, not in an emotional way, but in a laser-like, conscious, and precise way.

When we meditate, we begin to recognize our connection with this creative force, and we begin to know that we are part of this love, that we are the same as this love. We are infinite and eternal.

When we meditate, we become one with our infinite self. In our growing awareness of this higher self, we become much more than our personal self. We begin to recognize the magnitude, the beauty, and the infinity of who we really are.

CHAPTER 5

BY HEART

When we know something deeply, we feel it in every cell of our body. We know it literally by heart. We don't need to be reminded of it or shown it again — we simply know it. It's like riding a bike: once you've learned how, it becomes part of your reflex patterning. With a meditation practice, you begin to know yourself by heart. You learn about yourself inside and out — what you think, what you feel, who you are. A greater awareness of who you are reveals itself to you. The more of your eternal spirit, your real self, that you allow to shine through, the more authentic and original your life becomes.

Meditation helps you know your truest self, the part of you that never dies.

It doesn't matter if everyone you know thinks something is right — it doesn't mean it's right or true for you. As you learn to trust more and more in your sense of knowing, you become more confident of it. We all have a unique contribution to make, and only you can express yours in your specific way. No one else can really tell you what your contribution is; it's up to you to discover it within yourself.

Meditation helps you remember what you know. It takes you home.

Home is truly where the heart is. It is where love is. Love is an art, a great and powerful practice. It is something to use, to work, to be. It is a verb, an action. Every time we choose love we are affirming life. We so often make distinctions, such as, "I can love this, but not that." We draw lines. But love is consistent. It is constant and all-embracing. It is a state of "being in love" with everything! Deepening and broadening our practice of love is one of the greatest gifts of meditation. When you begin to know yourself by heart, you learn to truly love.

It doesn't matter what you think about love. It only matters *that* you love.

CHAPTER 6

COMING HOME

Everything is connected. Nature constantly reflects this truth to us. Physics and other sciences prove it over and over again. But you already know this for yourself when you remember your newborn child's eyes or watch the stars in the sky or feel your heart beat or hold your mother's hand or watch a hummingbird — love is all around us, and miracles abound in every moment.

Meditation acts like an accelerator in your life. Every area of your life will be touched by your meditation practice. Things will begin to change, to realign, to come into a new and better rhythm.

You will notice this right away. It will make you aware of what your next step is in life, at just the right time, in just the right order.

Things that you've been holding on to or suppressing will become more and more apparent to you as your meditation practice evolves, and as though a fog is lifting, you will begin to see the truth of where you are standing at this moment.

As you walk along your path, many things will come your way, easily and effortlessly. Various teachings and teachers and religions and books and experiences and ideas will present themselves to you in perfect order, in perfect timing — and all the roads take you home.

Trust yourself. Trust your journey. Your unique path is your own. The way you get there has its own perfection. Whatever you need will arrive at just the right moment. All you have to do is recognize it as it comes along. Meditation keeps you connected to yourself. It helps you recognize the many signposts along the way. It gives you a quiet, calm, and clear inner knowing that never fails to guide you on your path.

Meditation takes you home. It takes you to your heart's knowing. It guides you unwaveringly, unerringly to your next step. Meditation is an unfolding process that takes you where you are, as you are, and shows you — one spiritual foot in front of the other — the way home.

the practice of meditation

PART

TWO

CHAPTER 7

HOW TO PRACTICE

There are really only two things you need to be able to do to meditate: become aware of yourself and stay there for a while.

This formula is not only a simple way to practice meditation — it's also a key to life: to be mindful where you are, wherever you are; to become more and more conscious from moment to moment; to be your true self, in every situation, in every circumstance.

Meditation is simple and practical. In a curious way, it is as ordinary as it gets. Many people who try it at first don't think they are doing it right; it's so simple and unextraordinary, they think meditation must be something more complex or esoteric than what they're doing. Because people often think they are doing their meditation wrong, many give up doing it at all.

It is a practice. *Practice* comes from the root word *praxis*, meaning "to do action." You have to do the action for meditation to work. Every time you sit to meditate you are building up a *spiritual muscle*. The more you use it, the stronger it gets. It gains strength, agility, and capability over time. This energetic apparatus you build by meditating will absolutely change the way your life works.

Every time you meditate, you lay down another layer of consciousness, like rings in a tree trunk. Remember: the consciousness you make — conscious moment by conscious moment — is what you take with you when you die. It's part of your soul's accumulated knowledge, your soul's wisdom. It is the basis of what you are, and it becomes part of the continuum of your infinite self.

Remember: all you need to do is become aware of yourself and stay there for a while.

CHAPTER 8

CREATING
SACRED SPACE

Everywhere we are is holy. Everything is holy. Yet, some places have more spiritual wattage than others. When many of us decide over many years that a place is sacred, it becomes imbued with more sacred energy. We see and feel that these places exude holiness. Imagine a cathedral, for instance, created for the specific purpose of worship. The architects and crafters who designed and built it knew what its purpose would be. Every nail was pounded and every tile was laid by a person who intended the church to be holy. Then add the intention and devotion of the priests at its head, and all the vestments, rituals, and symbols of the ceremonies. Finally, add the congregation with all of their sincere beliefs and prayers. Multiply that by all the years of worship in the cathedral, and you can see how intention creates sacred space.

When we meditate we consciously create a sacred space. We can make any space sacred simply by deciding that it is sacred. By bringing our full consciousness to that place, we are imbuing it with our soul, and it becomes energetically transformed.

If you already have a part of your home that feels especially peaceful to you, that's a natural place to meditate. Any place where it is calm and quiet is a good place to begin. I often meditate on my balcony that overlooks the city skyline, but I have also meditated in bed, on the couch, and even in the bathroom because that was the quietest room in the house at the time.

The more you meditate in the same place, the more that place becomes imbued with peace. Just walking by it or even thinking of it will instill in you the quality of consciousness that you have invested there. By repetition, you build your own unique place of power and awareness — your own altar.

Remember this as well: even though you can empower a place to give you a feeling of sacredness, don't forget that *you* are the generator of that feeling in the first place, and you can take that feeling with you wherever you go. You can create sacred space anywhere.

CHAPTER 9

SITTING

The first thing you need to do to meditate is to find a comfortable position to be in so that you can sit quietly for a while. It's challenging enough to deal with the mind's complaining without having to contend with the body's problems as well. If you are uncomfortable, you won't be able to sit still, and your meditation will become a meditation on discomfort and tension.

Sitting cross-legged is the most common posture for meditation, but it is not essential to the practice; it is simply a comfortable position for some. Meditation originated at a time when people most commonly sat on the ground, but there are other reasons to sit cross-legged. These may become important as your practice unfolds, but the main purpose of a cross-legged posture is that many people find it relaxing and natural.

Again, the important thing is to be comfortable. Any comfortable sitting position will do. You can sit in a chair, on the couch, or against the headboard of your bed. You can sit on a park bench, on a blanket in the garden, or on a tire hanging from a tree. Be comfortable. If your spine can be straight as well, that is even better.

Over the years, I have worked with many students who for one reason or another can't sit comfortably, so I have them lie down. Even though this changes the energetic dynamics a bit, it still works. The only problem is that we are conditioned to fall asleep when we lie down, so you have to work a little harder to stay alert. However, since being comfortable is so important, if it feels like you need to lie down at first in order to become still, then lie down.

It really doesn't matter whether you sit or lie down — anytime you do anything in full consciousness, you are meditating. Conscious walking, conscious washing the dishes, conscious singing of a lullaby — it's all meditation.

Still, I like sitting. It works well, it invites less distraction, and it increases the likelihood of touching your truest self. Don't forget to turn off the phone and do whatever else you need to do to prevent interruption. You want to create the optimum conditions for a deep and authentic experience.

CHAPTER 10

BREATHING

Once you've found a way to sit, then begin to be aware of your breath. The breath is the bridge between the self and the soul; the more connected we are to our breath, the more connected we are to our soul. When we stop breathing, it means that in some way we are disconnecting from ourselves, from our feelings, from our life force.

Notice your breathing now. Are you restricting it in any way? Is it rolling naturally and fully? Does the chest feel tight? Does it feel open? The breath is a powerful barometer of our state of mind.

We may hold our breath when we're tense or when we're concentrating, nervous, or upset. If the breath is shallow, there is tension in the body. You might be surprised at how often the breath is tense — and worse, at how often you're barely breathing at all. When the breath is full and deep, it's a good indication that you are physically, mentally, and emotionally balanced. Watch a baby breathe, and you'll see the belly expand as she inhales and recede as she exhales. She is completely relaxed.

Take a deep breath. Notice how easily your whole being comes into a calm balance — just by taking a breath. The breath is like a wave: far out from the shore a wave begins to form... *inhale*...from the depths, a powerful, surging expansion forms and gains momentum, expanding and expanding, then it crests and curls, and finally...*exhale*...crashes to shore, dissolving into bubbles and spray as it begins to recede for its long journey back out to the depths of the sea again...*inhale*...

With the breath deep and full, your meditation becomes alive. It is in flux, like the sea. It is infinite and changing. When the breath flows, the mind opens, and we expand. The breath is the guide. The breath is constantly giving us feedback: time to move forward, time to stay still; time to listen, time to speak; time to be subtle, time to stand strong; time to hold fast, time to let go.

A breath is a complete cycle unto itself, self-perpetuating and constant. It is our life. It animates us. It is the first thing we do when we come into form; it is the last thing we do when we leave it. We don't have to try to breathe; it is automatic. It is a great mystery and a miracle. It is surrender.

Learning to listen to the sound and quality of the breath is the best teacher you will ever have. No one else can know for you where you are in your meditation. No one can guide you more surely or more intimately than the breath's subtle awareness.

Let the breath be your life's song. Learn the melody it is singing. Appreciate the harmony of it. Learn to understand and support the disharmony too. Your song is your own, and it is beautiful and unique.

CHAPTER 11

INTENTION

As soon as you choose a place to meditate and turn off the phone, you are setting your intention. Meditation is a practice in focus, concentration, and staying firmly with yourself. This is a tremendous act of will because generally when we first sit down to meditate we create a hundred reasons to get out of it. We find ourselves wondering about all kinds of things: *Did I put the dishes away? Did I return that call? That closet really needs a good cleaning out.* The distractions can seem endless.

It takes discipline, or as one friend of mine says, *blissipline*, to stay focused on spirit. The mind wanders to mundane things. But the blessings and insights that we get from even a five-minute daily practice of meditation are invaluable. We expand in a subtle but powerful way. We access something bigger than ourselves, a pure consciousness that leaves a deep impression. Setting our intention and sticking with it is the key that opens this vast realm of possibility.

This inner world is your private temple, your direct connection with grace. People often find it difficult to describe this realm because it is beyond words — literally metaphysical, beyond physical experience. When you try to describe your experiences of meditation, they either sound overly glamorous or incredibly subtle, and either way they are often misunderstood. But it isn't necessary to put them into words. Let it be your own private knowing. You need no validation from the outside; you are the only one who needs to know what your meditation has shown you.

Setting your intention to meditate secures your practice. Once you have this foundation in place, it creates an energetic touchstone that calls you back again and again.

CHAPTER 12

ATTENTION

One of the reasons it's important to be comfortable in your meditation position is so that you can allow yourself to rest in a state of relaxed attention for a while. *Relaxed* and *attention* may seem like opposing ideas, but it is the closest word combination that describes how to orient yourself in meditation: be relaxed and alert simultaneously.

Think of a cat sitting motionless, watching a butterfly move through the garden. Or think of a rooster standing quiet and relaxed in the perfect silence of the dark, alert for the dawn, receptive to that inevitable illumination of the first light.

Meditation is the decision to know ourselves as spirit, as soul. We create the conditions that allow for this process to take place. We create an environment that is conducive to getting to know the soul. Meditation gives us the opportunity to hear the song of our soul. It allows us to listen to that still, quiet voice within.

Whatever we give our attention to — everything we see, hear, feel, and experience — expands in our awareness and translates into our life experience. In meditation we get the opportunity to see what we are creating and to consciously reevaluate or recalibrate the choices we make. When we meditate, we are learning to be conscious of our thoughts. Most of our thoughts are a running commentary on what's happening around us and a recreating of our reality from moment to moment. When we sit to meditate, we become aware of how we are creating our reality and how we can reshape it as we go along.

One of the ancient teaching riddles a guru presents to a student to ponder is "Who is the thinker of the thought?" Meditation shines the bright light of our awareness onto the dark of our subconscious minds, the automatic pilot of our brains. We become aware of what was hidden. We begin to wake up from a dream.

CHAPTER 13

BEING BY YOURSELF

Most of us don't know how to be alone. We're afraid of the dark when we're little, and we're afraid of the dark in ourselves when we grow up. We learn to fill up all the dark spaces with TV and newspapers and drugs and busyness and anything we can think of, anything not to be alone. But if you can examine the word *alone* it comes from the compound word *all-one,* and there's a big difference between the words *alone* and *lonely*.

When we meditate we enter into ourselves. Sooner or later, we discover something very precious. We touch upon the diamond

50

of our heart. Sometimes there's mud all over it, but don't let that fool you — it's still a diamond. The mud is our shame, our pain, our beliefs of unworthiness and separateness. These are all common misconceptions of the ego. It shrouds our light.

When we meditate we discover that we are not alone. We find our deep connection to the whole of life, and we come to know that we are all one. We are loved. We are good. We are forgiven.

Every time you choose to be present, you become more aware of the most expansive, highest part of you. This ever-reaching ability is what makes humanity special. We reach. We aspire.

Look at how magnificent we are! We reach the stars. We fly like angels. Who else but us would try to fly to the moon? We are beautiful dreamers, seekers, visionaries, and inventors, and we change the world.

And best of all, we have the great capacity to wonder. That's what I love about us most. We wonder! We say *What if? Now what? Why? What's next?* We are always growing, endlessly evolving.

Meditation is filled with wonder. It is constantly spiraling us inward and upward, lifting us to higher and higher realms of understanding, creativity, and love. Meditation teaches us how to be present to the wonder of the moment. We sit, quiet and alone, but then we come to discover we were never alone at all. We are all taking this journey together — all finding our way home.

CHAPTER 14

COMMON QUESTIONS

In your meditation practice certain questions may arise. The following are the ones that most frequently come up.

How long should I meditate for?

If you are just beginning a meditation practice, I suggest sitting for five minutes a day in the morning or evening. This is an easy, doable practice. The point is to make a commitment that you know you will keep. If you choose a half hour, it may work for a few days, but then you may find yourself putting it off, and then you may miss a day, and then another day, and pretty soon you're not doing it at all.

You hear different instructions within different systems of meditation. Many schools suggest meditating for twenty minutes a day, but there are others that say you should meditate for an hour a day or more. All of these different systems are valid; all of them work. The two guided meditations on the CD included with this book are about fifteen minutes each. The important thing is to find a length of time that works for you and commit to it.

I encourage people to meditate for *some* period every day. The point of meditation practice is the practicing. It won't work if you don't do it.

Pretty soon you'll find you have an established meditation practice in place. When life gets challenging, you'll suddenly realize you have a secure inner position you can easily return to, a place where you can find your center again. As you continue your practice, you'll discover a wonderful thing: the more difficult things get, the more centered you can remain. When life gets hard, you'll no longer become as off-balance from the unpredictable circumstances around you. You will find instead that a great shift has occurred within, and you can calmly and clearly observe what is going on without being thrown off by it. You will find that all those simple periods of meditation have brought about a great inner change. You will no longer be at the whim of outer circumstances. You will have found a new sense of peace and freedom.

In that regard, there's no better time to meditate than in these difficult periods. During hard times I encourage you to meditate more often, not less, as this is when you need it most and when your practice will benefit you the most. This is also the time when you're most likely to stop meditating, so take care not to become distracted by the stress around you and to remain consistent in your practice.

When life gets challenging, try meditating once in the morning and once at night. You can listen to the meditations that come with this book or go back to your simple five-minute practice. It might seem like a short amount of time, but it will keep you on track. Or, if your practice has faltered, it will get you on track once again. Think of your meditation practice as a gift to yourself, not as a chore; those five minutes can save your life. They will enlighten and liberate you.

What do I do with my hands?

In the old teachings, meditators would put their hands in various positions called *mudras,* a Sanskrit word that denotes a symbol for a particular state of consciousness. If you touch the pads of your thumb and index finger together, for example, this is called *jnana mudra*, the symbol representing knowledge; the index finger represents the individual self, the thumb represents the universal soul, and together they symbolize the knowledge that occurs when self and soul join in meditation.

There are many ways to place your hands, each one having a different meaning and purpose. Some positions will come naturally to you, and the one you choose without even thinking is a perfect starting point. You can fold them or interlace them. You can rest them on your lap, palms up or palms down. You can put them together, softly laying one on top of the other.

Many new students instinctually start with their palms up. This is a position of receptivity, and it is a good place to begin. It says *I am willing and open.* You can try it now. Close your eyes and rest your palms facing up in your lap. Feel the sensations in your body and mind. Now turn your palms down. Can you feel the difference? Which feels more comfortable?

As you embark on your practice, notice what your hands want to do; trust that, and do that. It will be perfect.

What if I can't stop thinking?

Inevitably, new students come to me shyly at the end of a class or workshop and say, "I just can't keep my mind still. I keep thinking and thinking and can't stop my thoughts." I laugh and say, "Well, join the club. There's not one of us who doesn't experience this."

The mind's function is to generate thought. There would be something wrong if it didn't do that. Thinking is the function of the ego. It's always trying to figure things out.

The ego is so often misunderstood and unfairly represented. If we didn't have an ego, we wouldn't be human beings. The ego's purpose is to help us be in the world, and so it keeps thinking, all of the time, doing its job. It wants us to survive. It wants to keep us safe. It wants us to feel special. If we didn't have an ego, we wouldn't do anything at all. The ego isn't bad. It's the driving force that makes us want things and attempt things. It motivates us to compete and create and desire and go forth and live in the world. That's not a bad thing. It is a natural part of being human.

When you meditate, a great shift in consciousness takes place: you learn to watch your thoughts, instead of joining them. They are still happening, but you're not directly, emotionally involved. You're just sitting quietly, watching the thoughts. By becoming aware of your thoughts, you are staying present in the moment. When you are present to the moment, you are in a state of grace.

As you sit to meditate, you might start thinking about a conversation you want to have with someone later, but as you are meditating, you will notice that you're thinking about the conversation. The moment you become aware of this, the thought itself disperses.

The thoughts will keep coming. That's what they do. Think of them like soap bubbles, little bubbles of thought. A bubble comes up, a little world of an idea, like that conversation you want to have, and then you become aware of the thought, the bubble, and *pop,* you return to the space between the bubbles, between the thoughts, and you're fully back in the moment again. Then another thought will surely come, and *pop,* the process continues, again and again and again.

Over the millennia, there has been a vast amount written and taught about this, for it is essential to all meditation. There is a great yet simple discovery at the core of it: you are not your thoughts; thoughts are simply happening.

As you notice you are lost in thought, or caught in one of

those bubbles, then you become aware that you are, and *pop,* you snap back to this present moment, this breath, now.

Every time you do this you break the spell of illusion. You become your true self again. You realize that you are eternal and beautiful, and that realization becomes more embodied within you. You realize you have a soul, a vast spirit, and you become linked with it. Body, emotions, thoughts, and soul become joined.

You see, the process is simple. All you need to do is become aware of yourself and stay there for a while; recognize your thoughts for what they are, let them go, and return to the present moment again.

What style or tradition should I choose?

I like to find what's similar about things. I've studied many forms of meditation. I've loved them all for different reasons, but some resonate with me more than others. Yet the heart of meditation is the same, regardless of the form. It shows us our connection to all of life. It shows us our wholeness. It harnesses our egos to something greater, and it enables us to notice all the love that is present in every moment.

Which style or tradition you choose is a personal decision. The important thing is to find what works for you. You may be attracted to the formal majesty of Catholicism and truly enjoy rituals like communion, confession, and the rosary. Or you might find yourself drawn to the ancient traditions of Judaism, steeped in dynamic dialogue and beautifully sung prayers. Zen Buddhism may invite you with its order and simplicity. Or Hinduism, imbued with colorful and mythic ceremony, might be your heart's calling. Each system in its own unique way offers a complete spectrum of experience and a cohesive sacred path.

My aim is to show you the heart of meditation, and this practice will work with whatever tradition you decide to embrace. There's a precious diamond at the heart of meditation, just as there is at the core of ourselves, and it exists at the center of any style of meditation practice, no matter how different one may seem from another. The core element of meditation is love,

love in the highest sense, far beyond personal or emotional love. It is the life energy of the universe, an energy that is not particularly attached to anything, but is connected to everything. It is eternal and it is everywhere, without exception.

Whatever way your spiritual path leads, know that it is perfect. You may very well end up designing your own unique path, one that takes you a little bit here, a little bit there, letting your own inner voice guide you. Meditation can enhance this path, whatever it may be.

Meditation is not about religion or dogma or technique or perfection. It's about your spiritual journey. Your journey is unique and personal and holy. It will take you to the top of the mountain. Whether you use meditation in a religious context or you use it as a means to simply focus your mind, it is flexible. You almost immediately see and feel its benefits.

What if I'm not doing it right?

This is my favorite question. So many people think they're not meditating correctly. Inside the question is self-doubt, the belief that when you really, truly are yourself there is something wrong with you. This underlying presupposition can lead many spiritual seekers to give up their meditation practice. If there is one spiritual tenet you can be sure of, it is this: what we are at our core is perfect. We are holy. The way you meditate — your style, the way you experience every moment — is perfect too.

If I had just one message I could offer it would be *trust yourself.* Meditation gives you a way to know yourself and trust yourself, to authentically understand what you think, how you feel, and who you are. From this vantage point, you discover new ways of thinking, and you begin to fully contribute your own voice and sing your own unique song to the world.

What about meditating in a group?

I love meditating in a group. Remember the last time you were at a church or a temple...or a football game, for that matter? It's so easy to join in with group energy. You can glide right in.

If you imagine listening to a great song at home versus hearing the same song live in concert, you can sense how powerful group energy can be. Meditating with a group often produces a heightened experience. However, you can't meditate in a group all the time, and the value of meditation is in its daily practice.

There are places in the world like ashrams, monasteries, and convents where everyone is dedicated to the ideal of meditation in every moment. This kind of life can make it easier to stay on your path, but for most of us, that's not the life we have chosen. There are children to raise, jobs to do, educations to pursue, relationships to nurture, and on and on. Life asks us to participate, to be in the world but not of it. Meditation teaches us this unique balance of integrating our inner and outer life.

Whatever time you spend meditating on your own heightens your clarity and receptivity. Then when you meditate in a group, your deepened awareness becomes your contribution to the group. The group's experience will deepen because you are there. You affect the group, and the group affects you.

Can I ask questions in my meditation?

One of my favorite things to do in meditation is to bring a question into it. When I find I am worrying about something, I bring the concern into my meditation. All you have to do is introduce the idea, the circumstance, the person, the world event — whatever it is — into your mind, with the thought that you are open to seeing it in a new way. You will be amazed at the insights you get when you bring real-life problems into the laboratory of your higher mind. You really do know the answers already.

However, if you go in with a fixed idea, you'll come out with one too, so it's important to stay open and not presume the outcome. Resist the temptation to assume the answer before you offer it into the meditation, to plan the way you want it to turn out, the way you think it ought to go; this narrows the possibilities. Empty your mind, and see what comes up. You will be surprised by what you know.

How can I tell if what I'm experiencing is just my imagination?

Here's the bottom line. It's really simple and very important. When you are connecting to truth in your meditation, it will always feel like love. If there's criticism, doubt, anger, punishment, comparison, self-centeredness, arrogance, pride, self-pity, sorrow, pain, depression, resignation, fear, greed, envy, competition, pressure, laziness, righteousness, judgment, irritation, imitation, debate, confusion, dullness, numbness, or guilt, then it's ego, not love, and not true.

When it's true, it will ring true. You will know it because you don't have to work hard to remember it. You won't have to repeat it over and over in your head. It becomes a knowing instead of a thinking, and your meditation practice will deepen.

Should I focus on something?

There are many different focal points that you can use when you meditate. The purpose of a focal point is to create a point of concentration so your mind will wander less; it helps you to stay focused for the duration of the meditation.

There are traditions where the eyes are kept open — it's sometimes called gazing, where you look out into space but focus on nothing in particular. Some styles of meditation ask you to focus on an object like a candle flame, a flower, or even your own image in a mirror. Many traditions focus on the breath, with techniques including gently counting each breath or simply following the sensation of the breath through the nostrils as you inhale and exhale. Some traditions will have you focus on one of the centers of energy in the body called *chakras*. There are seven major chakras, and each one produces different results.

There are many other types of focal points as well, from imagining geometric forms in your mind to listening to the sound of the sea. All have a purpose, all are useful, all teach unique and specific positions of consciousness. Find the form that fits you.

Just as with the questions of how to sit or what to do with your hands, I advocate a personal discovery process, especially in the beginning of your practice. What you naturally are drawn to do will likely be your best starting place. Ask yourself what feels natural and right to you each time you sit to meditate.

If you are working with a teacher, she may suggest a particular focal point, or a word prayer called a *mantra*, or a hand position to use in your meditation. Use them and see what happens. There can be profound wisdom in a good teacher's intuitive guidance, and it may greatly accelerate your learning curve or lessen any resistance that might exist in you.

What if I see colors or images?

When we meditate it is common to see colors or images, hear sounds, feel sensations, or have entire conversations within ourselves. There is a quality of dreaminess that can occur in a meditation, and just as in a dream, we can create imaginary landscapes to fill the space of the meditation. Sometimes the brain gets bored and starts manufacturing all sorts of imaginary scenes to keep it occupied. This can be just a distraction, but sometimes it can be a significant part of the meditation.

A teacher may give an instruction, for instance, that brings your awareness to a certain focal point of the mind, and within it you may see the color indigo, or a point of pure light. This can be evidence of a certain state of consciousness, showing you that you are energetically in the right place.

Many extrasensory events can occur during meditation. It's usually best to not become overly attached to these perceptions; that way, you keep creating an empty tablet that allows for deeper levels of inner knowing to arise. Think of it as a chalkboard that you keep erasing to see what comes up next, beginning again and again with a blank slate. The extrasensory perceptions are not the most important part of your practice; rather, it is the quiet opening to your own inner wisdom that allows you to be initiated into greater degrees of expansiveness and love.

What about difficult states like worry and fear in meditation?

If you are in an agitated state — of anger, jealousy, or worry, for example — the best advice is to simply take a deep breath and *relax*. Keep breathing, deeper and deeper, and you will find that the tension slowly begins to dissolve. Underneath the agitation is a quiet stillness. If you stay in this place long enough, you will reach the knowing of what these uncomfortable states are trying to show you. Meditation will teach you to stay with these states of being until they reveal their true meaning. There is a gift inside any fear. Wait for it. It is a treasure.

What if I don't understand my meditation experience?

If I could give beginning meditators only one tip for their practice, it would be this: *be willing to not know for a while.* All of our greatest ideas and inventions, from the wheel to quantum physics, come from a willingness to dwell in the unknown until an insight arises.

True perception is the ability to stand in awareness, leaving aside all the thoughts that have been thought before. We have to be willing to *not know* for a period of time — sometimes a short time, sometimes a long time — and in this state of consciousness we can give birth to inspiring new thoughts and make quantum leaps in our practice.

What should I expect when I meditate?

When you meditate, most of what you experience will be ordinary — as ordinary as the night sky with a billion stars, as ordinary as a lone hawk's cry, as ordinary as language, as ordinary as a sunrise, as ordinary as the wail of a newborn's first breath.

Everything is ordinary. It's one ordinary thing after another. That's the magic of an ordinary moment.

The ordinary is sacred.

CHAPTER 15

A SIMPLE MEDITATION EXERCISE

Find a relaxing place to meditate.

Make your body comfortable in a position you can stay in for a little while, and close your eyes.

Let your body relax. Relax your shoulders, relax your chest, relax your stomach, relax your forehead.

Become aware of your breath. Notice if it's shallow or tense, and begin to even it out by letting the breath become deeper, fuller. Take several deep breaths through the nose until the body and mind begin to feel calm.

Soon you'll feel a physical sensation of being centered and an inner feeling of balance. Keep your attention steady. Allow your awareness to become still like a candle flame, gently flickering and constant. Become more and more still.

As thoughts come into your mind, let them pass like clouds in the sky. Don't become involved with any single thought, just allow it to go by. Any time you find your mind wandering or you become lost in thought, return to your breath again until you feel your mind and body come into balance once more.

Feel the stillness at the center of your being. Sense the vastness of all that is. Stay here for a while. Even a moment will make a difference.

This is the heart of your meditation. This is where you can bring your worries and fears, problems and plans, or just bring yourself without any agenda at all.

After a while, you'll feel a natural sense of completion. When you do, let your breath become more conscious again. Let it get deeper and fuller. Let your awareness move into the heart and spread throughout your body as you gently transition out of your meditation, opening your eyes when you're ready.

Now take this awareness into your day. Today is a new day and anything can be. Bring the gifts of your meditation into your daily life. Let everyone and everything be touched by your refreshed perspective. Look at everything with new eyes. See your partner, your children, your job as brand new.

◆ ◆ ◆

Meditation returns you to your inner source. Within you, every answer can be found. All you have to do is relax and open to the moment.

When you meditate, you discover new parts of yourself. Your inward exploration gives you access to new qualities of your being that you didn't know existed and reassociates you with parts of yourself that have been tucked away and forgotten. Each of us is so complex and beautiful. We are like a crystal with a thousand facets, each one a different aspect of our true self.

Our crystal can get muddied or covered up. Think of meditation as a polishing process. Imagine the light of your awareness touching the brilliance of your newly polished crystal. See how the light can shine through it as through a prism.

When we meditate we are connected to divine intelligence, and we discover that this greater perspective can guide us in every moment of our lives. We see how each step we take links to the last and is in perfect harmony with where we are at any given moment.

Whenever you have a problem or you're not sure of your direction, take a moment and do this exercise. When you open to divine guidance, you become permeable to the flow of universal wisdom. Whether it is a creative solution to a problem, a new way of looking at a difficult coworker, or the next line in a poem, you can tap into this enormous wealth inside you by quieting the mind and opening to creation.

CHAPTER 16

HOW TO USE
THE MEDITATION CD

There are two meditations following the introduction on the CD. The first meditation, "Opening," is designed to facilitate peace of mind. It can help you quiet mental restlessness, focus your thoughts, reduce stress, let go of worry, make enlightened decisions, and attain mental clarity. It can instill inner calm, empowerment, and strength during times of change and challenge. "Opening" can also get us back on track, reconnecting us with our creative flow, our purpose, and our path to enlightenment.

The second meditation, "Deepening," is designed to open and heal the heart. It soothes emotional pain. It stimulates and nurtures the process of healing and deepens your understanding of your infinite self. It adds emotional depth, quells angst, and provides deep relaxation and profound connection with all that is.

The two meditations are very different, and at different times you may find yourself drawn to one more than the other. Trust your process completely. Whatever works for you is right. Some find that listening to the introduction is a meditation in its own right. Also, try listening to the CD with headphones; the experience may be more intimate.

I hope you will use this program. It will change your life. The best gift you can give yourself is a little time every day to just be yourself and meditate. It is such a fulfilling process of discovery, and it is simple to do. I am happy to offer you this map to help you on your way.

Blessings to you on your sacred journey.

ACKNOWLEDGMENTS

My thanks to Adrian, for asking for this;

to Hans Schick, who listened to the CD in the making and
added his note and breath to it;

to Joel, who said just do it;

to Andrei, who loves me from forever;

to Marc Allen, for believing in this project;

to Michael and Judy, who are this book's fairy godparents;

to my mom, for being real and true and brave;

to my dad, for showing me the sun and the moon and the stars;

to my sister, Grace: well, you know honey, I love you beyond
words;

to all my students, who asked the questions and taught me
everything I know;

and finally, to my teacher Ari, who taught me well.

New World Library is dedicated to
publishing books and audio and video products
that inspire and challenge us to improve
the quality of our lives and our world.

Our products are available
in bookstores everywhere.
For our catalog, please contact:

New World Library
14 Pamaron Way
Novato, California 94949

Phone: (415) 884-2100 or (800) 972-6657
Catalog requests: Ext. 50
Orders: Ext. 52
Fax: (415) 884-2199
Website: www.newworldlibrary.com

ABOUT THE AUTHOR

Diana Lang is a "teacher's teacher" of meditation and yoga, with nearly twenty-five years of teaching experience. She is a spiritual counselor and radio personality, and she lives in Los Angeles, the city of angels.

You can contact Diana Lang through her website, www.dianalang.com.